Computers

by Maryellen Gregoire

Table of Contents

Consultant:
Adria F. Klein, Ph.D.
California State University, San Bernardino

capstone
classroom
Heinemann Raintree • Red Brick Learning
division of Capstone

Using Computers

Computers are everywhere. People use computers every day. They read on computers and do their work on them too.

People use computers to find information.

Communicating

Computers are connected to each other through the internet.

People can communicate with their computers. Emailing, texting and tweeting are ways to communicate on a computer.

You can send a letter from one computer to another.

You can use a computer to buy things. There are web sites that help you sell your things too.

Working

Many people use computers for the work they do.

Doctors use computers to help them take notes about patients.

Artists use computers to draw.
This artist is drawing a cartoon.

Students use computers to learn about a topic. Then they type reports to give to their teachers.

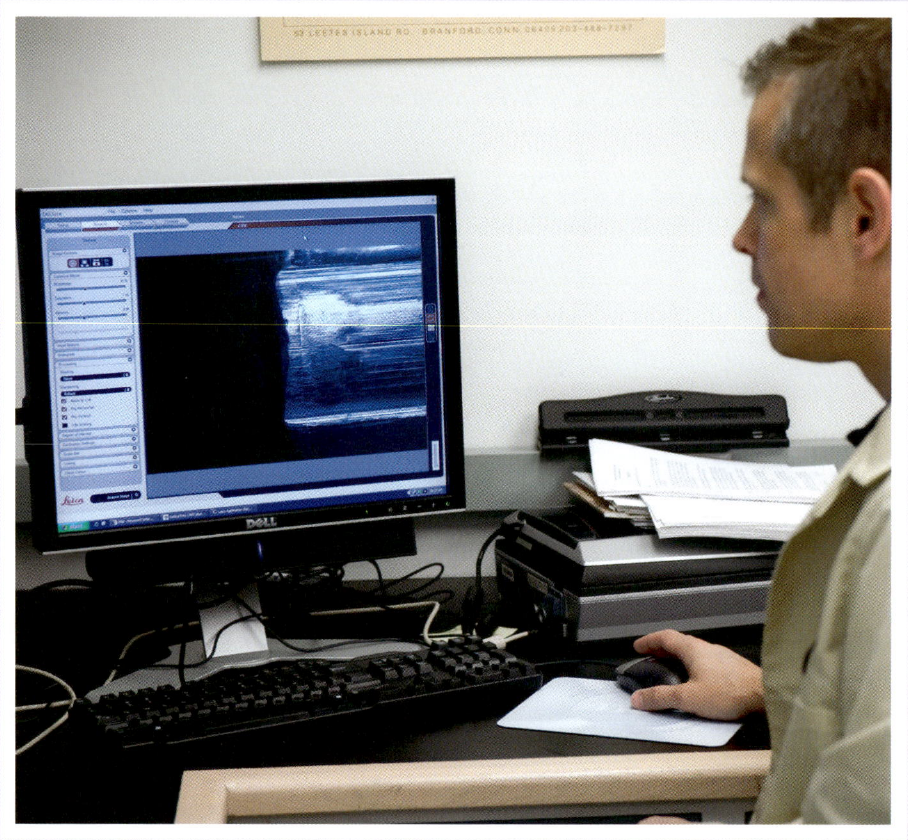

Scientists use computers to investigate crimes. This scientist matches a bullet to a gun.

Police officers use computers to find out about criminals.

Having Fun

Many things you use every day have computers in them. Computers help you stay in touch with friends.

You can read a book or watch movies on a computer.

Computers can give you a lot of information, but computers are for fun too!